THREE HEARTBEATS

ISBN: 978-1-916770-18-8

Collins Ashley

Dedications

This book is a true story and dedicated to all those, both two and four-legged, that were there for the joy and the pain. I'm thankful for you because the journey would not have been the same without you!

Acknowledgments

Thank you Katheryn, Aunt Janet, Aunt Karla, Unc, Pam, Wo, Kristi, Marie, Mara, and Patty for listening to the story and providing honest feedback! Many thanks to my trio of nieces for their youthful perspectives! A huge debt of gratitude to my mom for her help and guidance with this book and throughout my lifetime! Many thanks to my husband, Greg, for believing in me and encouraging me in the pursuit of happiness and fun!

Anna K. and Isabel were the best of friends!
They had a very special bond that was built over
many years. Time spent reading books, watching
tv and going to the beach were all fun because
Anna K. and Isabel were together. For 17 years,
Anna K. started and ended her days with Isabel.
They loved each other and were family!

Anna K. and Isabel met when Anna K. visited an animal shelter many years ago. Isabel was a sweet, grey tabby kitten with big green eyes! The years passed quickly and Isabel was no longer the young kitten Anna K. adopted. Isabel was now an old kitty who became very sick and died.

Anna K.'s heart felt broken. She was lonely.
She missed Isabel and knew it would take
time to heal and feel joyful again. The house
Anna K. and Isabel once shared felt very
empty with only one heartbeat.

As time passed Anna K. slowly began to feel better, but the house still felt empty with only one heartbeat. Anna K. had more love to share so she decided she would visit the animal shelter to meet homeless animals that needed a forever family.

One day after work Anna K. returned to the shelter she'd adopted Isabel from seventeen years ago. She was greeted by the friendly workers who told her to walk around and meet the animals. There were so many sweet cats and dogs to choose from. How would Anna K. ever decide?

volunteer

volun

She walked and looked and looked and thought. Anna K. hoped for girl kittens because she was close to her sister and loved her very much. She thought it would be fun for sister kittens to grow up together. Anna K. came around a corner and saw a kennel with four kittens. All of a sudden she felt a bit nervous!

volunteer

volunteer

16

Kind shelter volunteers greeted Anna K. and
told her that there were two boy and two
girl kittens in the kennel. One girl kitten was
a tabby cat with black and brown stripes and
the other solid black. With nerves and
excitement, Anna K. approached the kennel
to get a better look. She was able to hold
the little kittens for the first time!

As she held the soft, furry kittens, she felt like these may be the sister kittens she'd hoped and prayed for. The love she shared with Isabel had shown her that she had plenty of love to give. It was actually her love and bond with Isabel that made her want to adopt again. Anna K. and the kittens could be a family but would Isabel approve?

Anna K. believed Isabel would approve of her adopting the kittens because she knew she loved her and wanted Anna K. to be happy again. Adopting the sister kittens would not replace Isabel's spot in Anna K.'s heart. These two kittens would simply be more cats for Anna K. to care for and love.

ANIMAL SHELTER

Anna K. quickly went to the front desk to make plans to adopt the sweet kittens. She was told that she could come back for them in two days. Anna K. told the kittens goodbye and that she'd be back. She had to prepare for the two new additions at home!

Anna K. and her oldest niece got busy buying food bowls, litter and a litter box for the kittens. She also bought a scratching post and some fun toys. Anna K., her family and friends were all excited to bring the kittens home.

ANIMAL SHELTER

Two days passed and it was finally time to pick up the kittens! Anna K. went to the shelter and gave her name to the friendly man at the front desk. He made a quick call and the sister kittens were soon brought out in their carrier. It was time to go home!

28

The curious kittens had a lot of exploring to do in their new home. They also had many visitors to meet because Anna K.'s family and friends were so excited to meet them! The kittens loved to eat, sleep and play. Anna K. was happy but she still had one important thing to do. She had to name the kittens. What should she call them?

After much thought and discussion with the kittens, Anna K. knew their names! The striped kitten with white whiskers would be named Pixie and the solid black kitten with black whiskers Scout.

32

Anna K., Pixie and Scout were comfortable and happy. With each passing day, they were becoming a family. The house felt full and like a home again now that there were three heartbeats. Anna K. felt very thankful and blessed to have Pixie and Scout in her family and looked forward to the fun years ahead with her sister kittens!

About the Author

Collins Ashley is an experienced teacher, counselor and cat herder! She enjoys writing, spending time with her family and friends and traveling. Collins's love for animals started at a young age and inspired her to share her story in <u>Three Heartbeats.</u> She and her husband along with their fur babies live in Texas.

Printed in the USA
CPSIA information can be obtained
at www.ICGtesting.com
LVHW072259281023
762291LV00010B/35

volunteer

volun

14

30